# The Process of Wholesaling Real-Estate: A Simple Approach

By Mark J Curry

Copyright © 2019

Mark J. Curry

All rights reserved. No part of this book may be reproduced in any form without permission, in writing, from the author/publisher.

# INTRODUCTION

As in any business venture there is always risk. You could lose money. However, in real-estate wholesaling, you are going to make <u>no risk</u> deals. This book will provide a solid overview and teach you things that you can use immediately to get the ball rolling and to get your real-estate endeavor off the ground. Have fun with it!

**Question:** What exactly is real-estate wholesaling?
**Answer:** You get properties under contract and sell them to other real-estate investors for a wholesaling fee.

**Question:** Is a realtor's license needed to wholesale real-estate properties?
**Answer:** No. You will be using a licensed realtor to help you get properties under contract.

**Question:** Is wholesaling real-estate hard?
**Answer:** If wholesaling real-estate was easy everyone would be doing it. But, if you know what you are doing, it is really not a difficult process at all.

**Question:** Is wholesaling real-estate a get rich quick business?
**Answer:** No! But you can earn some good money if you are patient, and again, know what you are doing, and always doing your due diligence.

# GETTING STARTED

In a nutshell, you will need to have some knowledge in the following areas to begin your road to success in real-estate wholesaling: Cash Investors, Realtors, Property Listings, Repair Costs, Running the Numbers, Writing Offers and Negotiating, Assigning the Contract, and Getting Your wholesaling Fee. In some form, all of these areas will be covered throughout this wholesaling overview.

It is important to note early on that it will most likely take many offers to sellers to get a property under contract. Depending on how aggressive or how conservative you run your rehab numbers will surely affect the ratio of the number of offers you submit to the number of offers that are actually accepted. Keep in mind, though, that with real-estate wholesaling, you will always need to build your profit, or, Assignment of Contract Fee, into the numbers. Therefore, your MAO (Maximum Allowable Offer) will always be less when real-estate wholesaling, than if you were buying the property to rehab and hold (A Rental Property), or to rehab and sell (Flipping). Consequently, the ratio of the number of offers you submit to the number of offers that are actually accepted will be higher for a wholesaler, than it would be for an investor who is buying the property to hold it, or to flip it for a quick profit. The thing to remember is that this business, like most others, is strictly a numbers game.

With it potentially being so tough to get a property under contract, you are going to want to be well prepared for when a property is finally under contract, so that you will be able to pass the property on to another investor. With all of your hard work, you will definitely want to collect that well deserved wholesaling assignment fee. You are going to need a minimum of five to ten qualified cash investors to start, and increase that number to twenty, fifty, or even more, once you really get the ball rolling. Keep in mind that the more cash investors that you have on hand, the better the likelihood of assigning that contract to one of them. You will also want to have three to five qualified realtors working for you. When it comes up, and it will, each realtor will need to know that you are working with other realtors. The reason being is that realtors will want you to sign an exclusive buyer's agent contract, meaning that you cannot work with any other realtors while under this contract. **Do NOT sign it!** However, as another option, you can sign an exclusive contract for <u>each property</u> the realtor introduces to you. Therefore, if a particular property goes to closing that that realtor introduced to you, then that realtor will feel more at ease knowing that they will receive their rightful commission, and will increase the chances that they will work with you.

Three important tips to remember:
1. If you want to wholesale you have got to put in offers. Do NOT stand on the sidelines. Get into the game!
2. Do NOT ever treat a business venture like a hobby!
3. You do not need an LLC (Limited Liability Corporation) for wholesaling, but one is recommended for a buy/hold property (rental), or a buy/sell (flip). With anything real-estate related you will ALWAYS want to speak with a real-estate attorney and/or your accountant.

There are <u>Three</u> ways to wholesale in real-estate:
1. Bird Dogging
2. Assignment of Contract
3. Same Day Close


Remember: You are NOT putting any of your own money down. By not putting any of your own money down will results in absolutely no risk. Some ways that you will want to communicate with your clients:
1. Email
2. Text
3. Google Voice (You get a free phone number, with voicemail)
4. Business Cards

No matter which wholesaling method you are going to do, you need two critical components: a motivated seller and a cash investor. You, the wholesaler, connect, or bridge, the motivated seller and the cash investor.

**Question:** What is a motivated seller?
**Answer:** A motivated seller is the owner of a property who has to sell quickly. Maybe the property is vacant. Maybe the property has been on the market for a long time, 60 plus days. Maybe the property was an inherited property and the owner does not want to deal with the property taxes, the upkeep, etc. Maybe the property owner lives on the other side of the country. Maybe it is someone looking for a very quick sale because they have equity in the property and their hand is being forced – behind in their mortgage payments and/or property taxes. They don't want a foreclosure or sheriff sale, as they will then forfeit that equity. A foreclosure will appear on their credit report record for many years. There likely are other various reasons why a seller might be motivated to sell their property as quickly as possible.

**Question:** What is a cash investor?
**Answer:** A cash investor is someone you find who will actually be purchasing the property that you have secured under contract. Once you have a property secured under contract, you now have control as to what happens to that contract – you can either purchase the property yourself as a buy/hold or buy/sell, OR you can pass that property (wholesale) on to a cash investor.

# BIRD DOGGING

Bird Dogging is not my preferred method of wholesaling, but people make lots of money doing it. In a nutshell, you will still be using your cash buyer (investor) to purchase the property, and bird dogging generally looks for FSBO (For Sale by Owner) properties.

A realtor is not necessarily needed for Bird Dogging. You will need to determine the retail value of the property by using comparables, determine the cost of rehabbing the property to bring it up to retail value, and run the numbers. At that point, you will make a verbal offer to the seller. Upon verbal acceptance from the seller, you then get your cash investor and provide them with all the details of the property, but you withhold the property address until you get a signed Bird Dogging agreement from your cash buyer. At that time, you then can give your cash investor the property address. By withholding the property address until you get the signed Bird Dogging agreement will prohibit the temptation of a not-so-nice investor bypassing you and going directly to the seller and not paying you your well-deserved Bird Dogging fee.

You can create your own Bird Dogging agreement or find one online. However, it is ALWAYS recommended to have a real-estate attorney draw one up for you, or at least review the one you have created or got online. Your real-estate attorney will know of all your state's real-estate laws.

Your buyer (the cash investor) will then need to do their due diligence to make sure the deal is a good investment for them. If you have properly run all your numbers it will be a good deal. The investor will then need to write an offer to the seller (the cash buyer will have their own realtor and/or real-estate attorney to do this for them), provide the earnest money, and set up closing. The cash investor is to give you the closing agent's information, including the date and time that the property will close. Upon closing, you will get your Bird Dogging fee. If you have a good working relationship with your cash buyer, they may pay you your Bird Dogging fee upon the signing the Bird Dogging agreement.

# ASSIGNMENT OF CONTRACT

In Assignment of Contract wholesaling, you act as the "middle" person between the seller and the cash investor. Your job is to get the property under contract and then "Assign" the contract to your cash buyer, for a fee. You will use a licensed realtor to draw up the contract and to get the property under agreement (unless you are a realtor – then you can draw up the contract yourself). Most states have their own standard real-estate sales/purchase agreements.

If you are wholesaling via the Assignment of Contract method, it is not recommended to go after Short Sale properties (due to the length of time involved) or REO (Real-Estate Owned) properties, because most banks will not allow you to "Assign" a contract. However, there are two ways around that: one is that the property can be bought with an LLC, and then that LLC (the holder of the property) is sold to the cash investor. So, they will be purchasing your LLC, which contains the property. The other way is to do a same day/back to back closing, where you would close first with the original seller. Then you would have a closing immediately following, whereas you are now the seller, and the cash investor is purchasing the property directly from you. The second closing, the one from you to your cash buyer, will have included in it your fee (the original Assignment of Contract fee) for the property. Obviously, these two ways are more involved, but it does provide alternatives to get those bank-owned properties.

In the Assignment of Contract method of wholesaling, you will again need to have cash buyers/investors prequalified. These are the people who you are passing ("Assigning") the property, that you are finding and getting under contract, on to. You will need to know all the criteria that your investors are looking for (by qualifying them) in their investment properties. You are in essence shopping for them – finding for your cash buyer EXACTLY what they are looking for, and want. This is VERY important when wholesaling real-estate. You aren't looking for properties that you would want and think are good deals – you are finding properties that your investors want, based on THEIR criteria, and think are good deals.

Once you know all this information and what your cash buyers want, and who you will eventually be assigning the contract to, you will need to start collecting and analyzing property listings based on the needs of your cash investors. You can do this though any method of your choosing: realtors, FSBOs, online real-estate websites – any method that allows you to view lots and lots of properties.

Once you have found good properties that are in need of rehab (you determine this through property walkthroughs, or via online on properties that have LOTS of clear, detailed pictures), you will need to determine the cost of rehabbing the property to bring it up to market value. After you figure a relatively accurate rehab amount, you will then deduct this amount from the ARV (After Repair Value). The ARV is the market value of the property. The market value is determined by obtaining 3-5, or more, recent comparables (within 3 months of the sale date, no more than 6) and within ½ mile (no more than 1 mile) of the subject property. A realtor can get comparables for you from the MLS (Multiple Listings Service). Although comparables are the BEST resource to determine market value, other useful sites that might get you into the ballpark are Zillow and Eppraisal.

Next, you will need to figure in your investor's costs, as well as your Assignment of Contract fee, which will also be deducted from the ARV. This now gives you what is called the MAO (Maximum Allowable Offer), or, your wholesale offer that you will use to try to get the property under contract with the seller. The MAO should NOT be exceeded at any cost. A good starting point (beginning offer) is 95% to 97.5% below MAO. This allows wiggle room to negotiate an acceptable offer for both parties. It is also important to mention - feel free to offer an even lower starting offer than 95% of the MAO. One never knows just how low a distressed seller is willing to let a property sell for. The better the deal that you can get a property for, the more money you can charge, if you want, for your assignment fee. Keep in mind - even if you decide to not increase your Assignment of Contract fee, your cash investor will be very happy with the deal that you just brought to the table for them. Your investor will be VERY happy, and that will increase the odds that they will want to continue doing business with you. It is a win-win! Just remember again, to NEVER exceed the Maximum Allowable Offer. Never!

Now, when you have a property under contract that your cash investor wants (based off of your prequalification of them and predetermining the types of properties your investor wants), and that this property is a good investment deal, based on the numbers that you ran regarding the rehab costs, the investor's costs, and the Assignment of Contract fee, it is now time to go through your realtor and put in your offer. Some realtors still use the old way of, "come on in and sign all of the paperwork". I prefer to use realtors who will use an online program called DocuSign - where it is all done on-line and can be done from the comfort of your home office. It's a huge time-saver!

It is very important to realize that many of your offers will not get accepted on the initial offer, and many times, not even at all! It is completely a numbers game. Making offers on properties to targeted motivated sellers, properties that need quite a bit of fixing up to get the home to ARV (After Repair Value), can range from 40% to 50% below the property list price, and sometimes lower than that. Sellers do not like this. They think that they are being "low-balled". Nothing is further from the truth. Sellers fail to realize that they are getting offers based on the worth of a fixer-upper home to an investor – not what a realtor thinks the property is worth from a retail mindset. Many times the realtor will list a home for the price the seller thinks it is worth, and not taking into consideration the costs to fully rehab the property, and other costs as well. FSBOs are also notorious for this as well. Reality will eventually set in for the seller once the property sits and sits on the market for a really long time. Continue to keep watch on the property if your initial offers are not accepted. When a distressed seller becomes even more distressed and possibly become even more motivated to sell, go back and make another offer - 30-60 days after they rejected your previous offers. It is even ok to offer less for the property than you did the first go-around, and always remember to NEVER exceed the property's MAO.

The contract offer and acceptance ratio can tend to be very discouraging; ten offers to one acceptance, 15 to 1, 20 to 1, even 25 to 1, or more. Real-estate wholesaling is strictly a numbers game. The most important thing, other than to not exceed the MAO, is to keep submitting offers, over and over again. When counter-offering, it is ideal to have very good negotiating skills.

Once you FINALLY get that hard-earned property under contract (agreement), you pay the earnest money (down Payment - $500-$1,000). All the clauses (contingencies) in the sales agreement are to be waived (mortgage, termite, radon, lead-based paint, etc.), except one; THE INSPECTION CONTINGENCY. The inspection contingency gives you (and your cash buyers/investors) 10-15 days to inspect the property. Your investors likely will want their contracting crew to get a more accurate figure of the repair/rehabbing costs.

The inspection contingency clause is what gets you out of a deal if you cannot secure a cash investor for this particular property, or if some unforeseen repair (cracked foundation, asbestos remediation, major electrical repairs, etc.) is found that will greatly increase the rehabbing costs in addition to the original estimated costs for rehabbing this property. At this point, you can back out of the deal and get your earnest money back. This is why there is absolutely NO risk in real-estate wholesaling. The only thing that you will lose is your time and effort in getting this property under agreement – nothing else. Another option would be to renegotiate the additional repair costs, which would then reduce the previously agreed to selling price by the additional repair cost amount. If the seller does not want to reduce the selling price by the additional repair cost amount, you can then just back out of the deal and get your earnest money returned. If the seller DOES agree to reduce the selling price by the additional repair cost amount, an addendum to the sales contract will be needed. Remember, your realtor will be the one to fill out the sales agreement, make any changes to the agreement (the addendum), and submit your offers. Also in the sales agreement, the settlement date can be thirty days from the signing of the contract. If the cash buyer wants to settle sooner, the settlement date can easily be changed.

In real-estate, as with ANY business transaction, NEVER do anything via word of mouth/verbal agreement. A verbal agreement will never stand a chance if there is ever a court battle. Everything in real-estate MUST be done in writing.

Once the property is secured under contract and you have paid the down money, it is now time to contact your cash buyer, or ideally, cash buyers, as this is the time to market the property under contract to them. You will want to include anything you can about this property – good comparables (3 to 5 provided by your realtor), the repair costs, the price of the property (the SALE PRICE for the property, PLUS your Assignment of Contract fee), the amount of down money required, pictures of the property (as many as possible), number of bedrooms, number of bathrooms, square footage, and anything else that you deem important, such as a major repair, etc.

Once you have an interested cash buyer, you can then meet them at the property individually, or, you can set up an open-house if you have multiple investors interested in this property. You will need your realtor there to allow you access into the property. Make sure to have your Assignment of Contract with you and filled out. It is also recommended prior, to have any legal contracts that you use cleared by your real-estate attorney.

If one of your cash investors wants the property, they must sign your Assignment of Contract Agreement, which defines the property, the assignment from you to them, and the price of your fee. In addition, the cash investor needs to provide you with a Proof of Funds letter, as this will be forwarded to the seller of the property. Most sellers of real-estate transactions will want verification that funds are available to be able to buy the property. Lastly, once an investor signs your Assignment of Contract, you will be reimbursed of the initial money that you put down on the property. It is recommended to collect double the amount that you put down on the property. This way, if the cash buyer backs out of the deal and you lose your initial deposit, you will have made some pocket money for your troubles. Let the investor know that the earnest money down payment is non-refundable (this should be spelled out in the Assignment of Contract Agreement), and collect their money in the form of cash, or a bank check. When the property closes at settlement, you will get the balance of your assignment fee.

If you have multiple cash investors interested in the property, the first one who gives you a signed Assignment of Contract, a Proof of Funds letter, and the down money gets the deal. Or, use your skills to create a bidding war. If multiple investors really want the property, give the deal to the highest bidder – as in the one who gives you the largest assignment fee. Nice!

It is important to note that in any kind of deal, or transaction, that both parties are responsible to do their due diligence, run their numbers, verify that the ARV is accurate – double and triple check the cost of rehabbing the property, etc. At this point, if both you and your cash buyer happen to disagree on something, such as rehab costs, and it is under a few thousand dollars, the Assignment of Contract fee can be negotiated in the hopes to still get the deal done. A basic thought is that some assignment money is better than no assignment money. If changing the Assignment of Contract between you and your cash buyer ends up being the course of action, again, everything should be done in writing. If a compromise cannot be reached, then move on to another investor, or just back out of the deal.

From this point on, the cash buyer and his agents are responsible to get the necessary things completed prior to, and including the closing of the property. You assigned the contract – you are done. The investor is responsible to set up the closing and to give you the details – the name of the closing agent, location, date, and time. You are to provide the closing agent a copy of the signed Assignment of Contract Agreement (unless you actually got your full assignment fee from the investor when you signed the agreement with them). This way, the closing agent will know to provide you a check for the balance of the assignment fee. You can either pick up the check at the closing agent's office after the property has closed, or the closing agent can mail you the check. Congratulations!

Note: if you develop a good rapport with your cash buyers and/or do multiple deals with them, they may pay the entire assignment fee (as mentioned above) and the reimbursement of the earnest money upon the signing of the Assignment of Contract Agreement. That is up to both you and your investor to decide how the assignment fee will be handled –

whether you get paid up front or at closing. Nevertheless, the down money is always paid at the signing of the Assignment of Contract Agreement.

# SAME DAY/BACK TO BACK CLOSINGS

The wholesale process for Same Day/Back to Back Closings is very similar to the Assignment of Contract method of wholesaling. However, there are a few major differences and responsibilities that will affect you. You will still use a realtor. With the Same Day/Back to Back Closings method, you can now put in offers for REOs (Real-Estate Owned bank properties) and short sales. Dealing with the banks WILL be a much slower process, and the banks will not allow you to "Assign" the Contract.

Very similar to the Assignment of Contract method, you will still use your cash buyers and you will still get properties under contract that fits the investor's criteria – properties that THEY want to buy. From here, everything remains the same as with the Assignment of Contract: researching properties, finding the ARV (After Repair Value), using comparables from your realtor, doing your walkthroughs, determining the rehab costs, running all the numbers, and ultimately getting your MAO (the Maximum Allowable Offer for the property).

Like before, you will use your realtor to get a property under contract. Upon acceptance, you will need to put earnest money down as a down payment for the property. A good amount to put down is $500-$1,000. You will then market your property that is under contract to your cash buyers/investors. Unlike using an Assignment of Contract Agreement with your cash buyer as you would for Assignment of Contract wholesaling, you will need to use a Purchase Contract for the Same Day/Back to Back

Closings strategy of wholesaling. As with any real-estate document, it is highly recommended to allow a trusted real-estate attorney to review the Purchase Contract that you intend to use. The attorney may even have one available to you. It is very important that any and all real-estate documents abide by all the laws governing the area (state) in which you live.

After the Purchase Contract is signed with your cash buyer, you will need to get two things from them: earnest money (down payment) and proof of funds. Regarding the earnest money - collect double the amount that you initially put down on the property. Let your buyer know that this earnest deposit is non-refundable, and collect from them either cash or a bank check. This way, if the investor defaults and does not follow through on the deal, you have a little pocket cash for your troubles, because you will likely lose your down payment money as well – so you will at least get to pocket the difference. Also, make sure that you get a proof of funds letter from your buyer (cash investor). You need to make sure that they have the necessary funds available in order to close on the deal on the property.

As the buyer is doing their due diligence, you will need to set up the closing. Being that you are actually going to close on the property (the front end of the "Back to Back"), you will also have to provide to the seller your own proof of funds letter as evidence that you have the funds available to close on the deal (you will have to actually have this money temporarily available [until the second part of the "Back to Back" happens] in order to close on the property). After you set up closing, the closing agent should guide you through the process, letting you know what documents you will need to get to them and what documents you will need to get signed.

Follow up and follow through with your buyer all the way up to closing day to help ensure the smoothest transaction possible. In real-estate, especially at the closing table, unforeseen problems can happen – always be prepared for the unknown. Once you have your closing with the seller (you now own this piece of property), you will then have the second closing with your cash buyer. At this second closing, you will receive (or be reimbursed for better terms) the money that you paid to buy this property, in addition to your wholesaling fee. This second closing can happen immediately following the first closing, later in the day, or even on a different day. You will set up both of the closings with the closing agent. Obviously, the sooner you have the second closing, the sooner you will get your money back for the property and be paid your wholesaling fee.

Personally, I prefer the Assignment of Contract strategy, as it is a much simpler process on the wholesaling end, in my opinion. If you do not have the funds to actually purchase the property, the Same Day/Back to Back Closing method will not be an option for you. Either the Birddogging or Assignment of Contract strategies would need to be used in this particular scenario. However, if you do have the necessary funds readily available, it does allow you to be able to purchase REO (bank owned) properties; something that you cannot do with the Assignment of Contract strategy of wholesaling. The reason being is that banks will not allow you to assign a contract.

One nice thing with a Same Day/Back to Back Close is that your cash buyer (investor) will not be at the first closing, so they will not know the amount that you bought the property for; at least not until it becomes available to the public, either through county records or websites, such as Zillow. So, what you paid for the property plus your fee is what your cash buyer will be paying you. Therefore, if the property is a fantastic deal, you can generally charge more for your assignment fee. Your actual fee will be hidden from the cash buyer. Please keep in mind though that in a few months down the road this buyer likely will view what you initially paid for the property. If this particular investor thinks that you are being "greedy", they may decide not to do business with you again in the future. In my opinion, if the property is a fantastic deal for your investor, it should not really matter to you because you can be almost certain that this investor will unquestionably want to do business with you again. Unfortunately, not all people will have this frame of mindset.

# REALTORS

Realtors are a dime a dozen and can be hit or miss. Some are very good at what they do, and others are not. Some realtors are extremely eager and will hustle for you, and some are just downright plain lazy! You will need to find realtors who are highly motivated to work with investors, and who are preferably investors themselves. These realtors will better understand the investor process, and mindset, and have a better idea of the types of properties you will most likely want, and will know the right listings to send your way. You want realtors who will show you the types of houses that you want to see, saving you valuable time, and to provide you with good comparables to help you to be able to accurately compute the ARV (After Repair Value) – the MOST important number that you will need to be able to run the numbers in order to provide your cash investor a good deal.

Realtors have many resources, such as the MLS (Multiple Listing Service), in-house listings, and word of mouth listings, and can save you a great deal of time. Again, use realtors who have experience working with investors, as they will know the process of investing, the types of properties that you are looking for, and will fully realize that investing in real-estate is strictly a numbers game. Even better, find realtors who themselves invest in real-estate. This is VERY important and cannot be stressed enough. Many retail realtors do not understand the investment process and hardly understand the investor mindset. As investors, we are NOT putting in "lowball" offers. We are putting in offers on properties in their present state of condition. This is just something that realtors who are not investors themselves just never seem to fully understand.

Regarding property listings – realtors are very good at getting them for you if they know the exact criteria of the types of properties that you and/or your cash buyers are seeking. However, you CAN go to most any real-estate website, such as Zillow, realestate.com, Trulia, and others, and put into the search your criteria and have property listings emailed directly to you. It all depends on how much time and effort that you want to put in to determine if you want to find the listings yourself, have a realtor do it for you, or both.

You will need realtors to allow you access into each property to assess the rehab costs, as well as to show the properties to your cash buyers once you get a property under contract. You will also need a realtor to submit offers and to get the property under contract with the seller. You can either sign contract offers at the realtor's office, or they can email you the contract through a program called DocuSign, which can save you tons of time, allowing you to utilize that time to search for and to find more properties.

When searching for a realtor, you can search online for realtors who will work with investors, such as realtor.com. You can also call any broker's office and ask the broker himself/herself, the office manager, or the receptionist to refer you to their best realtor who works with investors. Word of mouth sometimes will go a long way. Once you get a realtor who will work with you, make sure that they ARE actually working FOR you! If the realtor is not doing the job that you want, or doing everything that you expect from them, fire them and move on to another realtor. Time is money, it is limited, and it is valuable, so do not waste time. Choose a different realtor who will work very hard for you. The realtor pool is extremely large! One VERY important note is that most, if not all, realtors will want you to sign an "exclusive buyer's agent" contract. They want you to be exclusive only to them – meaning that you cannot use any other realtors but them. DO NOT sign this document! Are they exclusive only to you? Of course not! You want the option to work with as many realtors as YOU want. Plus, you do not want to be tied down to only them for 90-180 days, especially if they are horrible! However, what you CAN do to give the realtor a sense of security is to offer to sign a contract that gives the realtor exclusive rights to EACH property that THEY introduce to you.

# GOOD WHOLESALING PROPERTIES THAT MOST INVESTORS WANT

The bottom line is that ALL investors want a great deal. Investors will do one of two things: fix it up and rent it (buy and hold), or fix it up and sell it (flip or flipping). When you are wholesaling real-estate properties, you are actually "shopping" for properties that your cash buyers (investors) want. So, each investor that you are working with needs to be "qualified". This happens by you asking them questions and finding out specifically the types of properties that they are looking to buy. The more precise the questions and the more details that you can get from each investor, the greater the odds of assigning the contract once you get that property secured.

Not in all cases, but the general rule of thumb is that you will be targeting low-end starter homes. These homes might include: single-family residential, $200k and under, 3-bedrooms, 1-2 bathrooms, and square footage of approximately 1500. Again, these are probably the most common types of properties your investors will be looking to buy. But it must be stressed again that you ALWAYS want to be looking for and wholesaling properties that your cash buyers are looking to buy. It might be a duplex, multiple units, a five-bedroom home, in a specific area of town, no more than $20k rehab, commercial property, etc. This is why you will qualify each cash buyer that you are working with. Most investors will want to make a 15% profit or more.

To greatly improve your chances to secure these properties, there are a few things to keep in mind. Properties that are in good shape and "nice" are likely going to be bought at, or near, full price by retail buyers who will probably live in the home. These types of properties, if priced correctly, will usually sell quickly. These are not wholesale properties.

As a real-estate wholesaler you will be targeting motivated sellers, sellers who are in a state of distress. Here are some clues to help determine if a seller might be in a possible state of distress: the property is vacant, the condition of the property is not very good, the number of days the property has been on the market is relatively high, and the property's price has recently been reduced.

Whether you are actually in the home or just viewing pictures online (if viewing online – make sure that there are many pictures, twenty or more, and that these pictures are clear and show every room in the property), a vacant home is a clear sign of a motivated seller. This DOES include a property that might be staged (the strategic placing of furniture to make the home "look" nice). You are specifically looking for properties that show no sign of occupancy. An unoccupied property could mean that someone is possibly still paying a mortgage. If there is no mortgage, there will always be taxes and utilities that have to be paid. A vacant property is one that you will likely be able to obtain at a reduced price, especially if the owner is really motivated to sell.

The condition of a property will surely affect the price. The more rehab that the property needs, the more likely the owner will be motivated to sell. Whether you find them in the heading or within in the description of a listing, there are key words, or "buzz" words, to clue you in on as to the condition of a property. Look for words such as, "cash only", "as-is", "handyman special", "poor", "needs work", "has potential", "needs TLC", "investment property", "price reduced", "bring all offers", back on the market", bring your imagination", diamond in the rough", and others. Looking at the condition of a property and focusing on key words found in the heading or the body of the listing can get you a great property at a much lower price.

Either a realtor can inform you or you can find on most real-estate websites, such as Zillow, and others, the number of days that a property has been on the market. Obviously, the longer a property has been on the market, the more motivated a seller might become in moving the property at a reduced cost. Anything under thirty days is worth waiting to put in an offer on. Waiting longer, 45, 60, even 90 plus days on the market, will likely benefit a better price, and a larger profit for your cash buyer. To be sneaky, sometimes a seller will briefly take a property off the market and then relist it again. This will reset the number of days on the market. Doing a little research on the property can usually help you figure this out.

A reduction in the price of a property is a clear indication that a seller might be motivated to sell. It is usually very easy to spot reductions on a property listing, again, by using Zillow, Trulia, Realtor.com, or whatever real-estate website that you choose to use. Most of the sites will show the new price after the reduction the old price. Sometimes the old price is shown, but crossed out with the new price. One downfall when a property is reduced is that when a price on a property is changed, it could reset the "counter" on the number of days on the market, and the property might actually appear to be a new listing. Do your research (due diligence) and continue to use the minimum of 30 days plus on the market rule to put in an offer, increasing the likelihood of getting a really good deal on the property.

These four criteria will almost certainly put a seller into a distressed situation, and possibly having to sell the property at a reduced price. It is best to search for property listings that show vacancy, are in poor condition, have been on the market for long periods of time, and have reduced prices. In addition, look for those key "buzz" words. These listing are out there and are the ideal properties to wholesale and to assign the contracts to other investors. These are generally the types of properties that investors want – but always remember to qualify them. These are the types of properties that will maximize profit for your cash buyers and will likely motivate them to want you to continue finding properties for them.

# CASH INVESTORS

What do you have to do and where can you go to find cash buyers (investors)?

Remember, as a wholesaler, you are "shopping" to find the types of properties that investors want. The more details that you can find out from the investor, the better you can pinpoint their needs and will then know what properties to look for and to get secured under contract. This, in turn, will increase the percentages of Assigning the Contract to an investor that you worked so hard to get under agreement.

Here are some questions that you might want to use when qualifying an investor in determining the types of properties that they want:

Find out <u>exactly</u> where they are investing – specific areas of a city? Are there areas to stay away from? Where?

Find out the types of properties they want – single-family, duplex, multi-unit?

What is their maximum price range for a property and their budget for rehabbing the property?

What characteristics are they looking for in a property - number of beds/baths, square footage, etc.

What is their profit margin and the number of deals that they can do in a month/year? Can they settle on a property within thirty days? This is why "cash" buyers/investors are used. Wholesaling real-estate is a quick process. Settlement usually has to be done in thirty days or less. Cash buyers have this money already on hand. There just is not enough time for someone to have to go through a bank to secure a mortgage.

Finding cash investors is relatively easy. Finding serious investors? Not so much. This is precisely why it is so critical to qualify the potential investors as best you can, and to get as much information from them as possible pertaining to the properties that they want. Some great places to look for investors are through Google and YouTube. Just search for "cash investors", "cash buyers", "we buy houses", etc. There are other places where you can locate cash investors; places such as, real-estate auctions (foreclosures and sheriff sales), meet-up, or through other online searches and ads, through the use of bandit signs, REIGs (real-estate investment groups), and by places that offer free advertising, such as Craigslist.

# REHABBING

There is no right way or wrong way to figure out rehabbing costs. The more that you do it, and the more properties that you go through, the easier and faster this process will become. Also, when you find your cash buyer, they and/or their contractor will verify, or modify, your numbers. If there is a discrepancy with your rehabbing numbers and with the cash buyer's rehabbing numbers, some negotiating may need to be done. This means that you will either have to reduce your Assignment of Contract fee or reopen negotiations with the seller. The investor could possibly decide to take the hit off their profit, depending on the difference in the amount of rehabbing costs, but that is unlikely. Quite possibly, you and your investor could split the difference. It all depends on the relationship you have with your cash buyer. Real-estate is all about relationships and negotiations so every transaction will be different.

Many wholesalers and many investors have just as many ways that they figure out their rehabbing costs. But generally, if the process is done correctly, both wholesaler and cash investor's rehabbing numbers should be within a few thousand dollars, at most, with one another.

In any rehab, there are common things that will get done on every property. However, depending on whether the property is going to be rehabbed as a rental or as a flip will determine the amount and the kinds of upgrades that will get done on each property. In every case, always figure on putting on a fresh coat of paint, using neutral colors. Plan to put in low-end flooring, which may consist of low-grade carpet and/or vinyl, or tile. Higher-end flooring will consist of higher-grade carpeting and/or ceramic tile. It is also a very good idea to put in new light fixtures and ceiling fans, and replace all light switches and receptacle outlets throughout the entire property.

Remember, even though the wholesaler is not the one who is actually going to be making these upgrades and fixes, their cash investor will be, and knowing what needs to get done is extremely important because the wholesaler IS responsible for initially determining the rehabbing costs, and they will need to be in close proximity to the rehabbing costs their cash buyer will likely get when they do their property walkthrough.

Unless the interior doors are in great condition, they should be replaced with six-panel doors, along with the hardware. When determining kitchen and bathroom updates, several factors may determine if a light update or full update is needed. If a property is going to be a rental, then a light, or partial, update will probably be enough. For a flip, a full kitchen and full bathroom update is the way to go.

For either a partial/full bathroom update, replace fixtures, light bars, and toilets. The walls will get painted and the floors will get updated. Some of the differences between a partial/full bathroom update might be a new tub surround versus tile, and painting the vanity versus replacing the vanity. Replace the medicine cabinet for a flip.

For either a partial/full kitchen update, replace the sink and the faucet. The walls will get painted and the floors will get updated. Some of the differences between a partial/full kitchen update might be laminate countertops versus granite countertops, painting the cabinets verses installing new cabinets, and scratch and dent appliances verses stainless steel appliances.

# THE PROPERTY WALKTHROUGH

Items to consider bringing to a property walkthrough are as follows: a property inspection form (create your own or do a Google search to find one to use, or one that you can modify to fit your needs), a notepad/pen, and a phone (that has a good camera, a flashlight, and a calculator). Every investor and contractor will have their own way of doing property walkthroughs. Again, create your own checklist/inspection sheet that works best for you. There are some good websites that you can use to find the average costs for repairs, including labor, for a particular location or area. Also, Lowe's is a great resource to use because they have the cost of an item or the cost for a complete package (ex. range, refrigerator, microwave, and dishwasher), in addition to the cost that they will charge to install everything. These resources, if used properly, can provide a fairly accurate cost of rehabbing a property.

Although there are literally hundreds of things that you can look for when doing a property walkthrough, and with various checklist s that can be found in doing so through online searches, a property walkthrough should be a flowing, time efficient process. Once the process is done repeatedly, over and over, a property walkthrough becomes easier and much quicker. With all that being said, the following areas and items in the paragraphs to follow should be evaluated in every property walkthrough.

Upon arrival at the property, it is very easy to do an outside inspection; especially if you are waiting for your realtor to arrive, or if they are working the lockbox to get you inside the property. Inspect the roof, the foundation, paint/siding, and the chimney if there is one. Check the steps both front and back, railings, decks, sidewalks, gutters, and fascia. Lastly, inspect the outside doors, the garage and doors if there is one, any other outbuildings, the fencing, and the landscaping.

Once you are inside the property, check the paint and the flooring. Keep in mind though, that paining and flooring will be completed as part of every rehabbing project. However, if there are major holes in the walls and the flooring, addition work will need to be done – adding to the rehabbing costs. Check the kitchen, including appliances, and the bathrooms. In many circumstances, it is the kitchen and the bathrooms that could make or break a deal, so put extra care into these two important areas. Check all doors including closet doors, windows and screens, lighting, and light switches and electrical outlets to make sure that they are working. All the light switch and electrical covers get replaced as part of the rehab. Also, be creative when doing property walkthroughs. Can an additional room or ½ bathroom be added? Can a wall be removed to open things up? Is there a way to add lighting, either naturally or artificially? The more properties that are inspected and walked through the easier it will become to answer these types of questions.

Lastly, check some of the bigger ticket items, such as the furnace, the hot water heater, the electrical box and the wiring (make sure that there is no knob and tube wiring), the outside A/C unit, sump pumps, and wells. You will also want to make sure that none of the pipes are wrapped with asbestos, as this would require remediation. Again, online resources are available to determine the cost to repair/replace these items.

# RUNNING THE NUMBERS

If you cannot fix a home with money, it might be a very good idea to just move on from this property. Examples might be if a home is next to a power station that is "humming", a home under electrical wires, or a home near an airport, etc.

ARV – (After Repair Value) – This is the value of the home after it is fixed up (rehabbed). The ARV is THE most important number. If this number is off, even a little bit, it will throw off the entire calculation. To obtain the most accurate ARV, retail comparables should be used. These can be obtained through a licensed realtor. Real-estate websites such as Zillow can also be of help; any website that allows you to view the sold and settled properties. A minimum of three (the more the better) recent comparables should be used – homes sold within the past 3-6 months, and a radius within ½ mile to 1 mile tops, of the subject property. Your cash buyer is going to do their due diligence and either check your comparables or have ones of their own when calculating their numbers, so having recent and accurate comparables is key.

When using comparables, you should always keep in mind that you are searching for similar properties to the property that you are wholesaling. The comparables should be similar in square footage, the same number of bedrooms and bathrooms, and the same style home (ranch, colonial, etc.). A realtor can run a CMA (Comparable Market Analysis) which will provide the most accurate ARV because this program will make adjustments and deviations between the subject property and the comparables. However, the problem is that running a CMA is time consuming and most realtors will not want to do very many, if any, if you are not doing enough deals to make running the CMA worthwhile for them. Helpful Hint: keep clear of "war zone" properties (violent crime areas). Do not use comparables for these properties, and definitely DO NOT buy them.

Running the actual numbers is a fairly simple calculation. Start with your ARV (After Repair Value using at least three good comparables). Subtract the profit that your cash investor wants to make, plus their costs. This total will likely be in the 25%-30% range of the ARV. Whatever this amount is, deduct this from the ARV. Next, subtract the repair/rehabbing costs. Then, take the profit that you want to make and subtract. The cash buyer will not want to pay for closing costs, so subtract another 3%-4% to figure in closing costs. This final amount that is left is called the MAO (Maximum Allowable Offer). You will never EVER want to exceed this amount when you make your offers or you run the risk of losing some, or all of your profit. If you want wiggle room to negotiate will the seller, then offer 95%-97.5%, or even lower if you choose, of the MAO, but NEVER EXCEED the MAO.

Upon acceptance of an offer, put down $500-$1,000 earnest money (you will get this money back from your cash buyer when you sign the Assignment of Contract Agreement) and then contact all of your cash buyers. The first one who provides you with a signed Assignment of Contract Agreement and reimburses your earnest money (remember to collect double the amount you paid - bank/cashier's check or cash) gets the deal. You can also hold an open house, if you choose, for all of your investors to attend. You are the one who decides how to pass along your wholesaling deal.

When you present the deal to your investors, via phone, text, email, or by all three methods, include the property address, the investor's cost to purchase the property (the price you paid for the property PLUS your wholesaling fee), your ARV figure based on your comparables, the sold and settled prices and the addresses of the comps that you used, the rehabbing estimated costs, highlighting the repairs and the rehab work that is needed, pictures of the property, the closing date of the property, and the earnest money needed to secure the property (double the amount that you initially put down). If you choose, you can also put on the date when the inspection period ends. This is normally 10-15 days (always ask for 15 days when negotiating the property) from the date of the executed contract.

Time is of essence from when you get the signed contract for the property to getting your earnest money and signed Assignment of Contract from the cash buyer. This is because the inspection period clock is ticking. REMEMBER, this is your out if you cannot find an investor to take on the property, for whatever reason. This clause in the sales agreement allows you to get your down money returned, and what makes wholesaling a no risk venture. But the sales agreement must be terminated within that inspection clause date – NOT after.

You do not need to appear at the closing if you choose not to go. You will, however, want to find out the name and the address of the closing agent so that you can provide them with your signed Assignment of Contract so that you can get paid. One alternative is if your cash buyer pays both the wholesaling fee and the reimbursement of the earnest money upfront at the signing of the Assignment of Contract. But this is between you and your cash buyer how you will get compensated.

Definitely worth mentioning once again – it is VERY important to mention the back out clause (contingency) that must be included in the purchase agreement in the event that you need to back out of the deal. It can be short and sweet such as, "this offer is contingent upon further inspection of property and/or approval of buyers' partners within 15 days of execution."

# FINAL THOUGHTS

I hope that you found this real-estate wholesaling overview very helpful. Thank you for purchasing this informational and educational book. Good luck in the future with your real-estate journey; wherever it may lead. Have fun and make lots of money!

Utilize all of your resources (phone, email, internet, text, regular mail, realtors, brokers, investors, tax advisors, real-estate attorneys, etc.) to secure the following: Cash Investors, Real-Estate Agents (Investor Friendly), MLS Listings, Advertising (Bandit Signs, Business Cards, etc.), Real-Estate Websites, Property Rehab Checklists, Estimated Cost of Labor and Repairs, Cash Investor Purchase/Sales Agreement, Earnest Money Agreement with Cash Investors, Investor Promissory Note (If Needed), Assignment of Contract, Calculating the MAO for Investment Properties, and Determining the ARV for Investment Properties.

As with anything that you get from the Internet or from another person, or source, it is highly recommended that you consult with your tax advisor and your real-estate attorney. Always do your Due Diligence in ANY and ALL business transactions. Best Wishes!

# DISCLAIMER

This is a general process on wholesaling real-estate, and there are absolutely no guarantees that you will be successful and/or make money. Other investors may have a different process that works for them. As with any business venture and investment opportunity there is ALWAYS risk. There are NO guarantees that you will make a profit, and it's always possible that you will lose money. Individual results will vary. This is because every person brings different levels of motivation and desire, individual capacity, business experience, and expertise. Each person MUST do their due diligence. This book does NOT guarantee results and success. You assume ANY and ALL risk. The author, publisher, Amazon, and any of their affiliated partners are not liable or responsible for the outcome of any positive or negative results, successes or failures that are directly or indirectly related to any information in this book, as well as the writing, the printing, and/or the downloading of this book.

# ABOUT THE AUTHOR

Mark J. Curry earned a Bachelor's Degree in Elementary Education with a mathematics concentration from East Stroudsburg University, located in East Stroudsburg, Pennsylvania. He also earned a Master of Education Degree in Elementary Education, also from East Stroudsburg University. Mark is certified in grades K-6, and also obtained his mathematics specialization certificate for grades 5-8. He has taught basic arithmetic through algebra 1 and Geometry, as well as pre-secondary science in a New Jersey State prison since 2007. Mark has a daughter, Alexa, and a son, Landon. Daughter Abigail went home to be with the Lord shortly before her birth, in 2007.

Mark is also a real-estate investor on the side. He owned multiple properties and managed them for fifteen years. Mark obtained his real-estate license in 2003. After a lengthy break, Mark is back into investing in real-estate. His current project is the creation of a non-profit organization that will offer housing to low income families.

www.ingramcontent.com/pod-product-compliance
Lightning Source LLC
Chambersburg PA
CBHW030739180526
45157CB00008BA/3244